Samuel J. Donaldson

Lyrics and Other Poems

Samuel J. Donaldson

Lyrics and Other Poems

ISBN/EAN: 9783744711258

Printed in Europe, USA, Canada, Australia, Japan

Cover: Foto ©Thomas Meinert / pixelio.de

More available books at **www.hansebooks.com**

LYRICS

AND

OTHER POEMS.

LYRICS

AND

OTHER POEMS.

BY

S. J. DONALDSON, Jr.

PHILADELPHIA:
LINDSAY & BLAKISTON.
1860.

HENRY B. ASHMEAD, PRINTER

TABLE OF CONTENTS.

	PAGE
Eternity of Poesy,	9
Song—With a Bumper of Burgundy,	15
The Dance of the Stars,	17
Nature and the Soul,	19
Sonnet—On the Harp,	23
An Invocation,	24
Sonnet—To Lili,	27
Lines—An Analogy,	28
Sonnets on the Final Judgment	30
Song—"Where have the Mighty Fled?"	33
The Morning Hour,	35
Sonnet—On the Return of a Fair Young Lady to her Friends after a long Absence,	38
Youth and Age,	40
Lines,	45
To The Wild Rose,	48
Sonnet—On the Reasonableness of Death,	50
Sonnet—On Individuality,	51

Lines,	52
"Oh! would I were a Star, Love!"	54
Sonnet—On Friendship,	56
Song of the Fates,	58
Lines,	60
Lines to Miss J M. W.,	62
Song,—"Time is Gliding on,"	63
To Lili,	64
On Feeling,	66
Daphne and Strephon,	68
Theory of Creation,	70
The Falling Star,	73
To the Farmers,	74
To Amoret,	76
Dialogue between the Poet and his Lyre,	79
Eternity,	98
On Feeling,	100
The Universal Heart,	104
Hymn to the Catholic Church,	106
Sonnet on Chatterton,	109
Determination,	110
The Hermit,	112
Song—"Who Loves not to Gaze,"	115
Lines to Miss R. L. N.,	116
Sonnet,	117
Sonnet to Mrs. Fanny Kemble,	119

INDEX.

	PAGE
LINES—"MY HEART EXPANDED LIKE A FLOWER,"	120
TO LILI DURING HER ABSENCE,	123
LINES TO MISS S. W.,	127
THE LITTLE CLOUD,	129
LINES TO MISS G. C.,	134
SONNETS TO CONSTANCE,	136
LINES IN THE SPIRIT OF UNIVERSALISM,	139
"FAIR LILI'S HEART'S THE TENT OF LOVE,"	142
TO AMORET,	143
THE DEAD,	145
LINES COMPOSED AFTER AN ILLNESS,	147
LINES DEDICATED TO OUR HOUSE OF REPRESENTATIVES,	150
LINES TO MISS N. S.,	154
THE DEATH-BED,	156
NATURE'S VOICE,	158
BALLAD—"WITH LILY-WHITE HAND," &c.,	165
TO THE EXILES OF ITALY,	168
LINES ON UNFORTUNATE LOVE,	170
ON GENIUS,	173
TO AMORET,	175
TO MIRIAM,	178
TO MY IMPULSE,	180
AMBITION,	184
AMELIA—A FRAGMENT,	186
SPRING—AN ANALOGY,	204
ONE'S OWN DAY-DREAM,	206

Poems.

ETERNITY OF POESY.

They tell me blind Maeonides is dead!
That the sad Muses, bending o'er his bier,
Draped with the withered hopes of fallen man,
In sable garments chant the cycles sere;
Whilst pale-browed Nature mourns her wonted voice,
So musically pensive in the past,
Now hushed forever in one sepulchre.
Has beauty failed? Needs then the soul no tone,
That, varying with the tumults of the breast,

May speak for spirit in each changeful mood;
Whilst that a complex universe in forms
Of innate loveliness, and joy, and life,
May pass before it in a heart-review?
Who dares to say one heart can fathom love?
Or Being Absolute! Or deathless thoughts,
Which weave their fancies but in god-like souls,
And, when once born, are clustered like the stars
In the vast universe of mind expressed,
There to attract—repulse—and pour mild rays
Of intermingled radiance upon Hope,
The child of Consolation and Desire!
Who—wandering in sweet rhapsodies of soul,
Stealing unconsciously, like twilight dreams,
Into a heart of innocence and peace—
Oft gazes with devotion on those orbs,
All negligently sprinkled as they are

Throughout the infinite of Thought and God;
Then pines to add one voice unto that choir
Of sister spheres and spirit-wanderers.
Oh! I had thought the human heart divine,
And dreamt how waters of the spirit steal
Thro' winding chasms, and thro' darksome glens
From source as inexhaustible as God;
And I had dreamt of thoughts unutterable,
And glorious visions which no tongue may tell;
And I had dreamt how loveliest joys are veiled
From the far piercing eye of prophecy,
In the dim future of an untold age,
When light shall circle Spirit as a crown,
And e'en Maeonides shall be forgot,
And tuneful Milton wake the groves no more.

They tell me blind Maeonides is dead,
And that great themes shall thrill the world
    no more!
Then must the heart be dead! Lament the
    dead!
For in its beauty, and for depth of love,
I had supposed it infinite as God!

Ah! Many souls, enchained, are bound to
    Earth
Thro' beauty only, and the warm desire
One day to view the universal heart
Bloom like a flower; that as leaf shields leaf
From over moisture or too fierce a beam—
When that a heavy dew may drip from
    heaven,
Like distilled nectar from the feast of gods,
Crowning the jeweled cups fair Earth up-
    rears

To catch the shower; or the keen noonday
   rain
Of amber-shafted light may pelt the buds,
Reeling beneath the stroke in fainting
   dreams—
So heart, close pressed to heart, may soon
   display
The principles of union innate, where
Naught save harsh discord e'er hath reigned
   before!

I tell thee aspirations shall not die!
Tho' sympathy denied may waste the breast
That longs for a full echo to its sighs,
Yet, Nature, lost in utter loveliness,
And reveling within excess of charms
And power to please all such as come to
   her,
Can never waft a longing to the past!

The present fair;—Earth's future gleams with
    hope
Of joys superior to mortal range,
And thought extended to vast realms of mind,
Unknown, undreamt of in the cycles dead.

SONG.

WITH A BUMPER OF BURGUNDY.

Here's to the lady of my love!
The brilliant phantasies divine,
Which flow from mingled love and wine,
Might angels move!
No seraph-lyre in languishing
O'er azure fields, could ever bring
The tenderness,
Of sunny memories to the soul,
Such as flash sparkling from the bowl,
In hours like this,
When every sigh is light, and every dream
    is bliss!

Here's to the lady of my choice!
Each languid pulse in constancy,

Shall warm with love at music's sigh,
And lend its voice!
Tho' forms of heavenly mould and brightness
Blend winning grace with airy lightness
To charm the eye,
Whilst 'wildering labyrinthine streams,
Whose spirit-waves enhance earth's dreams,
Glide listless by,
No angel-form may please, when Amoret is
    nigh!

THE DANCE OF THE STARS.

Have you never heard the voices of The
    Night?
Come and hearken to them call
To the gaudy train of stars,
As they crowd unto the ball,
In a band of serried light,
At the bidding of the laughing Queen of
    Night!

Mark them tremble in their eagerness of
    heart!
While the lively pleasures throb,
How their sandals twinkle, twinkle
In the dance, unto the sob
Of the wind, that plays the part
Of the lute, the noisy viol, and the harp.

Like the echo of an everlasting thought,
See them flash upon the eye,
In that giddy whirl of glee;
Catch the music of that sigh—
For the soul, of Nature taught,
Should awake responsive anthems of the heart!

Thus the universe is solaced of its woe;
For heavenly tears are bright
As the soft descending shower
Ever glancing into light;
They glide, singing as they go,
Like the laughter of the rivulets—their flow.

NATURE AND THE SOUL.

In the sunlight of the morning,
Ere the shadow steals its slow step
From the meads, and dewy valleys,
To the boundaries of the mountain,
And its deep-indented chasms;
When the twin lips of Aurora
Breathe naught save immortal fragrance,
Wafting life, and health, and freshness,
O'er the flower-clad boughs and blossoms
And the wild wind woos so wildly,
And, in passing sighs and murmurs,
Speaks with such true heart and feeling
Of the wonders of Creation,
That all ope their leaves to listen,
As to faery tales of wonder;
Till, that lost in love and longing,

They would fain conceal their blushes,
Tho' they know not how to hide them;
When the light wells in the fountain,
As it weaves its sparkling fancies
'Neath the steadfast eye of heaven,
As tho' born of earth and darkness;
Go thou—muse upon thy Being,
Thrilled with deep, eternal yearnings
Of the everlasting Spirit;
So that in the calm of nature,
Thou may'st summon up before thee
Bright and never dying raptures;
Thoughts which bow deep souls with yearn-
    ings,
Everlasting heart-repinings
That their thoughts are not revealed.

They would paint them, and not speak them;
They would roll full tides of vision

'Neath the approving gaze of Heaven,
That the eye of all might see them;
They would weave enduring fancies
Out of aery clouds of nothing,
Like the castles of the sunset,
Or the purple ridge of mountains,
Or dissolving tints of rainbow,
Or the waving groves and willows;
Thus their dreams would be revealéd,
Like the thoughts of the Eternal.

Go thou—in the hush of Spirit,
That the still small voice of Reason
Deeply moving pure emotions
Of a soul that is immortal,
May like a clarion wake thee
Unto great resolves and daring.

Go thou!—Burst the bands which bind us;

Mingle freely with the sunlight,
Till thou lose thyself in Nature,
And its dream-life be revealéd
To the eye and to the reason;
To the ear and to the feeling;
That the darting spray and sunshine,
And the gentle sigh of Evening,
And the calm still joy at sunset,
May be more unto the spirit
Than mere signs and painted baubles—
May from henceforth be—a feeling.

SONNET.

IN THE UNAWAKENED MELODIES OF A HARP.

What soothing symphonies of sound and soul
Lie slumbering here, lulled in the lap of sleep!
Thus must they slumber, till a master sweep
The echoing chords. Then in wild surges roll
The thrilling raptures; under soft control
Of kingly art, we hear them laugh—or weep;
While to sweet rhapsodies of spirit, leap
The trembling pleasures, mingling sense with soul!
Thus in the heart lie sleeping, lost in night,
A mild variety of shifting dreams;
Each wayward thought, too fancifully bright,
Thro' Nature's half-raised veil in softness gleams,
Waiting in eagerness for reason's ray
To pierce the clouds, and roll the mists away.

AN INVOCATION

TO GENTLE THOUGHTS, THAT THEY MAY DWELL IN THE BREAST OF MISS M. P.

SPIRITS fair, which intertwine,
   Dreams of being, far above
Brilliant phantasies of wine—
   Milder strains than earthly love;
     On you I call—
     Come one, come all!

Wafted on the spicy air,
   From the realms of dream-land, come!
Come in varied forms, and fair;
   Make her breast your constant home;
     In numbers rise,
     Light up the skies!

AN INVOCATION.

Well I know the human heart
    Can endure excess of light;
Tho' a dull and sullied part
    Of the chain of being bright.
        Haste! raise the pall
        That darkens all!

Shadows drear have fallen o'er
    Human hopes and sympathies;
Hearts which ne'er knew grief before
    Now link hour to hour with sighs.
        Disperse the shade
        Despair has made!

Nothing nobler well might be,
    Than the sinner's heart renewed,
Thro' the grace which makes us free,
    And the mild Redeemer's blood.
        Forgiveness bring
        From mercy's spring!

Should our God full pardon give
    For offences foul and dark;
And in mercy bid us live
    Henceforth lives of heavenly mark;
        Sweet strain for strain
        We'll lisp again!

All unpracticed in the art
    Of the melodies of heaven,
We will tune the grateful heart
    To the strain—" We are forgiven!
        Glory to God,
        Salvation's Lord!"

Haste to lift the cloud that veils
    Heaven's deep mysteries from the sight;
Each pure spirit, joyful, hails
    Earth's redemption to the right.
        E'en in her fall,
        God's all in all!

SONNET.

TO LILI.

Most pure my love, tho' it despiséd be!
As a sweet violet, at midnight born,
Droops languishingly ere the gentle dawn
May smile upon it—such my love for thee;
Such the dim yearning of my heart for thee.
E'en thou shalt feel for me when joy has gone,
And the lithe spirit, of its beauty shorn
Shall wildly revel 'midst satiety,
No longer glancing heavenward with the eye
Of prayerful utterance, for the lovelier thought
Written upon thy brow; of its own sigh
From the fair palaces of dreamland brought
Heavily to Earth—in anguish there to die!
Sorely heart-stricken, there to bleed and die!

LINES.

As some dark water, struggling long with night—
Pent deep within the bowels of the earth—
Breaks thro' the trampled green, and wells to light,
A choir of languor bubbling to the birth;
The first wild tumult of its dashings past,
The softened cadence floating o'er the vale,
In dying murmurs still is fain to last
In the light echoes of the awakened dale;
So unto God,
Th' Eternal Lord,
The yearnings of the soul are known;
Each burning thought,
From Nature caught,
Is wafted upward towards his throne!

LINES.

As the wild rosebud wantons with the air,
    Then pines to find its sweetest fragrance
        shed,
Till bent with anguish and oppressed with care,
    It droops to mingle ashes with the dead;
As one by one its leaves forsake their stem,
    Hope whispers ever, when drear death be
        past
Their much loved fragrance may return to
    them,
    Tho' scattered on the pinions of the blast;
        So with the heart
        That's forced to part
With each dear rapture earth has given;
        Tho' crushed it lies,
        And bleeding dies—
It dies to seek new joy in heaven!

TWO SONNETS

ON THE FINAL JUDGMENT.

I.

FORTH from their spirit-sleep, the sheeted
    dead
  Bestir for judgment at the angel-blast;
  That shrill alarum, ushering in a past
Dark-lined with memories to bow each head
In guilt's humiliation, strikes a dread
    To every heart. With some, such pang
      shall last
  Forever—from mild Jesus' presence cast—
'Midst gnashing teeth, racked on tormenting
    bed,
    Deep-set—inflammable; where scorching
      rocks

Frame donjons huge; rearing their horrent
    front
  One mass of flame, and formed of fiery
    blocks,
Forced by machinery of howling winds
To keep such shape as best lost souls confines
In grounds thro' which heart-'wildering ter-
    rors hunt.

II.

And ye, ye blessèd, crowned with glory's
    wrēath;
  Now ye, rejoicing, hymn the Saviour's
    praise;
  Earth's mild Redeemer; great in all his
    ways!
Man—whilst with man he dwelt—a God in
    death!
Immortal anthems languish on each breath,

Whilst spirit-wavelets rolled thro' endless days,
Chant low the limitless eternities!
The heavens, fair arched above, the depths beneath,
Awake to ecstasy at that sweet sound,
Soft issuing in a chain of linkéd sighs;
Light silvery murmurs from the spheres rebound;
Each starry sentinel in slumber lies—
Lulled by the flow of those heart-melodies—
Or in its orbit reeling, whirls around.

SONG.

Where have the mighty fled?—
  The lords of spirit, and the souls of song!
For it doth seem to me,
That every godlike aspiration's dead;
  Earth has been crushed too long;
In vain, firm manacled, would Will be free!

Where have the mighty fled?
  The wrinkled ages smile at us in scorn;
Each hag her distaff plies,
Seeming to say, " 'twere better to be dead,
  Or even not been born,
Than that the soul should waste her power
        in sighs!"

Where have the mighty fled?
  Sad Earth disowns a race degenerate!

In sable garb and weeds,
She mourns her offspring in her first-born
    dead.
  Time may his hunger sate,
On such as ne'er enacted godlike deeds!

Where have the mighty fled?
  Their tuneful echoes cry from Earth to God,
"It must and shall not be!
For souls redeeméd have with anguish bled
  That we should hug the sod:
Earth and her languages shall yet be free!"

Where have the mighty fled?
  Deep, deep inurnéd in the human heart,
Their sainted memories pure,
Tho' to the past indissolubly wed,
  Shall with each life-drop start,
Since age but hallows them, and cries—"En-
    dure!"

THE MORNING HOUR.

For in the morning hour I have gold in my mouth.
Jean Paul Richter.

WHEN, from the dreams of night,
Eyes ope to view the light
Stream thro' the lattice bright
   Bathed in mild splendor;
Oh! how the radiance soft
Bursts on the spirit, oft
Bearing the soul aloft
   Past life's surrender!

Lost in the dreamy past,
Pleasures that ne'er could last,
Mist-like obscure and cast
   Shades o'er the reason.
When thro' the realms of old

Wings the free heart and bold,
Life leaves the earthy mould
  Chilled for a season;

Woven of subtle thought,
Dream-forms of air are brought—
Loved ones long vainly sought—
  To the pure vision;
Soon one mild image bright,
Drinks in the amber light
Cloud-like, and woos the sight
  To scenes Elysian!

Oh! how a halo steals
O'er the 'wrapt soul, and heals
Wounds which the wan heart feels
  Wedded to anguish!
Mildly a spectre-hand,
Waves to the shadow-land,

Where strains of spirit, grand,
   Soothingly languish!

But when the shadows steal
Till crushed beneath the heel,
Suddenly warm thoughts congeal,
   Light forms have vanished!
Dragged once again to earth
Home-thoughts cling round the hearth;
Dead to a nobler birth,
   Mild dreams are banished!

SONNET.

ON THE RETURN OF A FAIR YOUNG LADY TO HER FRIENDS AFTER A LONG ABSENCE.

We welcome thee as we would welcome Spring,
   Rosy awakener of the slumbering flowers!
   Thee, Time obeys; the "lazy-pacing" hours
Quickened of thy clear thought—the mellow ring
Of thy soft laugh—flash swiftly on the wing,
   Besprinkled with the perfume and the showers
   Which, gentlest exercise of all thy powers
With other joys, has never failed to bring!
While absent, every heart has yearned for thee
   As for a charm, which once possessed, had fled;

But, tho' bereavéd, yet it could not be
   That we should think of thee as of the
      dead;
E'en in remembrance too much life was left
For us to mourn sweet sense as so bereft.

YOUTH AND AGE.

HOW AGE IS DEPENDENT UPON THE TRAINING WE RECEIVE IN YOUTH.

Youth! youth! youth!
With a heart that leaps to life,

Age! age! age!
With a pulse that's ebbing fast;

Youth! youth! youth!
When the spirit sounds to strife,

Age! age! age!
When our hopes and fears are past!

Youth! youth! youth!
When its fervor warms each scene,

Age! age! age!
When the soul has lost its power;

Youth! youth! youth!
When each landscape's gay and green,

Age! age! age!
When darkness rules the hour!

Youth! youth! youth!
When the heart throbs wild with love,

Age! age! age!
When fairy dreams are banished;

Youth! youth! youth!
That forgets its God above,

Age! age! age!
When Earth's loved forms have vanished!

Youth! youth! youth!
With its sighs, its tears, its pains;

Age! age! age!
With its calm and peaceful hour;

Youth! youth! youth!
With its winds, and storms, and rains;

Age! age! age!
With its mild refreshing shower!

Youth! youth! youth!
With a spirit wed to right,

Age! age! age!
With its victor-palms and glory;

Youth! youth! youth!
That looks to God for light,

YOUTH AND AGE.

Age! age! age!
Its crown, the head that's hoary!

Youth! youth! youth!
With a hand to aid the poor,

Age! age! age!
With a heart yet young and tender;

Youth! youth! youth!
That with grace still strives for more;

Age! age! age!
Longing for Life's surrender!

Death! death! death!
With a hand so stiff and chill;
Death! death! death!
Of the sunken eye and low,—

Death! death! death!
Thou art both joy and ill;
Death! death! death!
Thou art both friend and foe!

LINES.

More than disconsolate—
  Hated of her I love,
Blackening looms my fate
  Where'er I move!

Music held mystic sway
  Long, long within my breast,
Chasing pale care away,
  Whispering—"rest."

Now that mild hope is fled,
  Stifling, a life-despair
Hisses—" tho' joy be dead,
  Still is she fair!"

Ne'er shall heart-longings wake
  Rapture as pure again—

Heart-thrills for her sweet sake
   Mingled with pain!

Robbed of my earnest youth,
   Fooled of my aim in life,
Still has she left me Truth
   Ruling the strife!

Singly to her I cleave,
   Feeling that "God is Love;"
Earth's fleeting joys I leave
   For bliss above!

Could I have sinned at all
   'Gainst beauty half so rare,
Know that death's gloomy pall
   Soon hides despair!

Man, tho' he reach to age,
   Dies ere they bare the tomb—

Life's fool—the white-haired sage—
   All seek their home:

Life's joy is waked of death;
   Death is but change of form;
Mingling in one quick breath
   Either can harm!

Maiden, so learn to live,
   That when you come to die,
No thought may anguish give,
   Waking a sigh!

TO THE WILD ROSE.

Sweet flower so pure and white
   Thy life is fleeting fast,
Each breath thou drawest breathe low, breathe light,
   For it may be thy last!

Apart from storms and strife,
   Protected from the gales,
Thou shadowest forth my dream of life,
   Amid the scented vales!

Each velvet leaf's a page
   Of dream-life unrevealed,
From glowing youth to wrinkled age
   God's law thy lips hath sealed!

TO THE WILD ROSE.

Perchance, were language given
    To lisp dream-thoughts to earth,
The incense wafted up towards heaven
    Would hallow lowly birth;

For as I look on thee
    Still-grows the thought divine,
The lowly soul's humility
    Is shadowéd forth in thine;

And as thy dreams are known
    To spirits pure and fair;
So does the Lord our God, alone,
    Judge human hearts thro' prayer!

SONNET.

ON THE REASONABLENESS OF DEATH.

The soul of Music murmuring in a shell,
   Wearied of Ocean's roar, longs for the land;
   When rolled of kindly fortune to the strand,
Borne lightly o'er the bosom of a swell,
O what sweet tremblings from its spirit well!
   Heart's silent dreams to melodies expand
   With that new being: tones and feelings bland
Gush with a rapture as thro' magic spell:
For harmony, dependent upon change,
   Resembles man in Life's monotony,
Pining until mild Death enlarge the range
   Of innate faculties and reason high!
The dread of dissolution seems most strange
In souls immortal, wed to harmony!

SONNET.

LAW OF INDIVIDUALITY AS EMBODIED IN THE PHILOSOPHY OF SCHELLING.

FOREVER and forever roaming free
   The infinite of Being, there shall fall—
   As heretofore to numbers musical—
A power enshrouding mind thro' law-decree
In forms of less or greater brilliancy!
   Thus Light wells as from a spring original,
   Weaving its gauzy net-work over all
The broad expanse of Nature's wavy sea!
But as those splendors die and fade away
   In graduated links of beauty's chain,
   The glories paling ne'er return again,
Nor those enwoven there forever stay!
The gloomy shroud is stern necessity—
The rosy smile, mild Being's passing ray!

LINES.

Oh! who can paint the burning cheek
    When sorrow, mingling with despair,
May find no deeper tone to speak
    Its anguish to the air!

The glow of love and shame, diffused
    O'er many a pale and careworn brow,
Betokens how a heart abused
    Still cherishes its vow!

What tho' the pensive ear of Night
    In silence drank those thrills of love,
Which were to last whilst circlets bright
    Should weave the dance above;

The soul that thirsts for happiness
    Is oft misguided in the way,

And dreameth not that deep distress
    Shall crown the close of day!

Then steel the heart to passion's call;
    Ah! let not Love's delusive voice
Cast over youth's fair dream, the pall
    Of a misguided choice!

"Oh! were I a star," he sang within his heart, "I would shine upon thee; were I a rose, I would blossom for thee; were I a sound, I would press into thy ear and thy heart; were I love, the happiest love, I would dwell therein. Ah! were I only a dream, I would visit thee in slumber, and be the star, and the rose, and love itself, and vanish only when you awoke!"—*Jean Paul Richter.*

Oh! would I were a star, love,
   That I might pour o'er thee
Soft trembling lines of silvery light,
Which, sliding down their pathway bright,
   Might turn thy glance to me!

Oh! would I were a rose, love,
   To paint my leaves for thee;
Mild pencillings of melting views
In changeful rainbow-tints and hues
   Should warm thine heart for me!

Oh! would I were thy heart's love,
   I'd thrill the purest breast,
That ever waked a balmy sigh—
When none save God and heaven were nigh—
   Or hushed its snows to rest!

But were I but a dream, love,
   I'd wing my way to thee;
Thro' all the realms of Nature sought,
The star, the rose, the secret thought,
   Should nightly blend o'er thee!

SONNET

ON FRIENDSHIP.

Love, admiration, friendship, are not bought!
   Unlike the sordid gems exhumed from
       Earth,
   These flash their sparkles at the lowly
       hearth,
Whilst kings have mourned to view their
       rays depart.
Compared to Friendship's recreating power
   How vain the rapturous thrills of eager
       sense!
   How kindly, praise and love's sweet in-
       fluence
Encircle with new charms life's fleeting hour,
Till heart, impassioned, wills each joy to stay!

These, like swift gleams of lightning, may
    not last;
Winged of the sudden thought and laughing
    eye—
A joyous train—they seek a smiling past,
Fair ushering into everlasting day
A mind imbued with love's eternity!

SONG OF THE FATES.

Twine, sisters, twine—
Sisters three,
Fatal three—
Threads of human destiny!
This for the living,
That for the dead;
Weave in a strand of memories fled;
Twist them together to form one thread,
Till the cord becomes a chain—
Galling chain—
Coiling round, and round, and round,
Heart and mind, till each is bound,
And the living wish they were the dead!

Twine, sisters, twine—
Sisters three,

SONG OF THE FATES.

Fatal three—

Threads of mortal destiny!

Here's for the living,

Here's for the dead,

Weave in a strand of hopes unfed;

Twist them together to form one thread,

Till that life becomes a misery—

A sigh—

Welling up, and up again,

From the heart-spring to the brain,

Till the living wish that they could die!

LINES.

Why do I mourn? No soul is near;
Earth lends no sympathetic ear
   To drink the strain!
The boundless fields of buoyant air;
The wide expanse of forests drear,
   But mock my pain!

Once 'twas not thus! No lark so gay
When morning blushed, or closed the day
   His tranquil eye;
Then dreams came quick as moments fled;
But lay these memories with the dead—
   I too would die!

From earthly joys—from charms of sense—
An all discerning Providence
   Would wean my mind:

LINES.

Why mourn we thus for what is not?
The past, when past, should be forgot,
   Or reason blind!

Is there a witchery in the strain
Sad memory wakes, tho' borne with pain
   And silent tears?
Who would resign one memory,
Sad tho' it be, for pleasure's lie
   Thro' manhood's years?

Nature shall be the solacer
Of myriad woes; unnatural fear
   Of what may be,
Vanquished, shall wander far away;
Nature alone shall be the stay
   Of age for me!

LINES TO MISS J. M. W.

Say, would'st thou have my spirit wear
A chain both sore and hard to bear?
Show me a maid with light brown hair!

A chain of sighs, whose links are tears,
Fast riveted of hopes and fears,
And thoughts which bow a soul for years!

But, should she add a hazel eye
That liquid melts, tho' none be nigh—
My heart is thrilled with ecstasy!

And, should the chiseled lip be there,
Which, statue-like, breathes one rapt prayer;
Immortals! say!—what is so fair?

SONG.

Time is gliding on,
Like a river—like a river;
The moments that have flown,
Have flown forever—ever!
No wave may backward roll
With the deep impulse of soul;
The seed each heart has sown,
Are sown forever—ever!

Life is winding on,
Like a river—like a river;
Each winged thought once flown,
Has flown forever—ever!
We may ne'er recall the past,
Or make the present last;
The deeds each soul has done,
Are done forever—ever!

TO LILI.

When I gaze upon thy brow, Lili,
    And see the artless smile
        Illume thy face
        Of matchless grace,
    Which seems to know no guile;
I ask with tearful eye, Lili,
    Could man but view thee now,
        Who 'neath the sun
        Could picture one
    So bright, so true as thou, Lili;
    So bright, so true as thou.

When I gaze upon thy brow, Lili,
    And note the artful smile
        Steal o'er thy face,
        Of faultless grace,

O'ershadowing it the while;
I ask with saddening tone, Lili,
   Could man but know thee now,
     Who 'neath the sun
     Could image one,
So light, so false as thou, Lili;
   So light, so false as thou.

LINES UPON FEELING.

I know not what my heart would say,
Yet shall my impulse have its way;
Pure feeling should be unconfined,
And freed from trammels of the mind.

Reason may echo problems brought
From her own realms of tangled thought;
But feeling never yet has found
An instrument her depths to sound.

What feeling is, and how it moves
The spirit that pure spirit loves,
Must ever rest as unrevealed,
As kindred truths to reason sealed.

The life within us hides its form
From frequent gaze; no curious charm

Can pierce that veil which dazzles sight,
Or drag its glories to the light.

But when the favorite hour has come
In spirit ecstasy to roam
Forth thro' great Nature's wide domain—
Reason may call, and call in vain.

Feeling, her own and truest guide
To pure expression, will deride
Such feeble shackles as would bind
The loftiest soarings of the mind.

When feeling holds her faery court
Imagination wings each thought;
When intuition claims her sway,
E'en reason stoops, and must obey.

DAPHNE AND STREPHON.

FAIR Daphne's linked in friendship's chain,
    But Strephon sighs for love;
Tho' oft he breathes the amorous strain
    No prayer that heart can move.

One dewy morn, when all alone,
    Not dreaming Daphne's nigh;
He thus begins his fate to moan,
    And waken sigh by sigh:

"Ah, Daphne! cruel maid!" he cries,
    "Why wound a constant breast;
Wilt still reject tumultuous sighs,
    And wrong a flame confessed?

As oft as I with burning cheek
    Would breath love's warm desires,

Thy rosy lips of friendship speak,
    And wake the smouldering fires.

But now, since tears may ne'er avail
    To ease the careworn heart,
The lightest craft that hoistens sail
    Shall me and Daphne part."

"Ah, silly swain!" a soft voice cries,
    "How long must Nature prove
That when a handsome gallant sighs,
    Maids mean by friendship—love!"

THEORY OF CREATION.

WHAT time Almighty will indued with form
The crude and ill digested elements,
(Which heretofore, thro' endless ages past,
Strove to combine in numbers musical,)
Æther, fair Nature's prime material,
Was moved to hear his voice. Thence light
    was born—
Bright tension of the one original—
And Time first throbbed his seconds to the
    glance
Of myriad and well directed spears
Hurled thro' thick darkness—tilting at the
    void
Which rolled before them moulded to a sphere
Impenetrable; shrouded from the rays
Glancing in colors from the upturned shield

Which guards the heart of envious Nothing-
   ness.
Thus first the glories of Eternal Mind
Were wove in language, which, to speak direct
To every heart that loves the beautiful,
Was syllabled from alphabet of stars,
That all might read who chose. But he who
   would
Falsely traduce this language of the soul,
By interlining truth with falsity
On Nature's manuscript, must inly pine
God's work's so far removed; feeling heart-
   pain
That others, innocent of malicious schemes,
Will read with joy the thoughts imprinted
   there;
Existence of a God immutable,
Whose pleasure, character, and name, is
   Love;

Whose life is circled of one principle—
The power of being loved by those He loves;
Whilst Reason acts thro' high creative Will
Able to mould all being to all forms,
With Wisdom's self to guide that Will aright.

THE FALLING STAR.

'Twas eve—a summer's eve—and starlight
 reigned;
But my fond heart throbbed to a higher key
Than that of Nature in its loveliest strain—
For at my side shown Beauty idolized!
A lady of the mildest grace and form,
Walked arm-in-arm with me, whose love-lit
 eyes
Streamed thro' the night, and bade the dark-
 ness flee.
So soft their radiance, that the stars looked
 down,
Longing to catch sweet Music's deeper soul;
One, stooping too near earth, in eagerness
Of love's unutterable ecstasy,
Encroached upon the orbits of her eyes,
When, lost in brilliancy, it sank to night!

ADDRESS

TO THE FARMERS, WHO, PRAYING FOR RAIN, WERE ANSWERED BY A THUNDER GUST, WHICH WORKED THEM AN INJURY.

Ye have your wish, ye men of wheat,
    Lean horses, pigs, and cattle;
The winds of heaven in conflict meet,
    Ranged valiantly to battle.

For three long weeks in sunny June
    Ye wrung your hands in anguish,
Beseeching God to send rain soon,
    Lest corn and plenty languish.

Now that the muffled skies are black,
    And spirit-drums yield thunder,

Whilst lightnings stretch the eye on rack,
   Ye own too late your blunder.

Your corn is beaten to the plain,
   Stark crazed with fright your cattle;
God's whirlwind champions ride amain
   So valiantly to battle.

But while ye mourn, the deep-souled sky
   Behind the dark clouds laughing,
Shall celebrate Eternity—
   Immortal sunlight quaffing;

Soon Earth's warm smile shall greet the eye—
   The threatening storm-clouds sever;
The rainbow-arch of victory
   Hangs over earth forever.

TO AMORET,

UPON THE MARRIAGE OF HER SISTER.

ONE smiling eve, slow step I turned
    To where the Santee flows;
  The dewy valleys clothed in green,
  Lay glistening with silver sheen,
For in the blue the planets burned
    As Cynthia fair arose!

When, lo! just near I chanced to spy
    A sweet-brier blooming fair;
  Each opening bud with promise smiled,
  Whilst those full blown, in radiance mild,
As tho' to tempt a passer-by,
    Swayed gracefully in air.

TO AMORET.

Such beauty waked the warm desire
    To win one to my hand;
  With critic glance I gazed on all;
  When, lo! I heard a footstep fall
That warned me in swift haste retire,
    And at a distance stand.

A handsome stranger won his way
    Straight to the fragrant tree;
  My heart beat loud with anxious fear
  Lest that fair glory disappear—
Plucked hastily and borne away—
    Which won my heart and me.

But, ah! so various is the taste
    That reigns o'er mortals' choice;
  His sleeve but dashed the roseate dew,
  In reaching for a flower, which grew

In beauty near, so pure and chaste
    It bade the eye rejoice.

Thus, Amoret, I feared thy grace
    Might win a wooer's eye;
  But he o'erlooked thy beauteous birth,
  And stooping nearer to the earth,
Became enamored of a face
    That beamed in radiance nigh.

DIALOGUE BETWEEN A POET AND HIS LYRE.

I.

When first I raised the trembling lyre
   And swept with transient touch the strings,
To wake the lay of soft desire
   Or soothe the sigh that sorrow brings,
Faint Echo caught the lingering strain;
   Ere yet its tremblings died away,
The soft vibrations breathed a name
     That woke anew the slumbering lay;—
        'Twas thy name, Mary.

II.

And still its tremblings answeréd low
   Responsive to the name it waked,

And movéd all to music's ebb and flow,
    Flooding both hill and dale, green sward
        and woodland lake;
Whilst ofttimes it a sinuous course would take
Thro' caverned rocks, and briary-brambled
    brake
Which gave back sigh for sigh, and throe for
    throe;
Whilom all nature gushed with one heart-
    melody.

III.

Cease! cease thy murmuring!
Or would'st thou break my heart?
Canst not impart
Some other whisper to the distant hills?
Nay! Greece with all her rills
Could never echo half so sweet a strain!
Then sigh again!

IV.

What would'st thou have me sigh?
That joy must die!
That all the loved and beautiful of earth;
That white-robed purity and worth;
That great thoughts teeming to their birth,
Are as the incense on the air—
A moment here—a moment there,
Or as " the wind that idly passeth by?"

V.

Nay, stay thy hand! That well known theme's
    too sad,
And one brought nearer to the heart of man
By the slow lapse of silent centuries!
It courses, fiery-pulsed, along his veins,
With every beat which times life's destiny!
Each second views the burning flood glide on
In eddying circles toward the source of life;—

With noiseless flow, pouring its fire-lapped
  waves
Around the anguished heart, which, half
  subdued,
Fainting 'neath excess of ceaseless wavering
'Twixt hope and fear, ever is ill at ease,
Until with power adverse it pours it back
To ebb forever in a reckless whirl
Along the parched and dried up arteries,
Flooding each separate organ linked to
  thought:
Nay, sing not that!
Each soul's its own musician for that strain;
'Tis the silent music of man's being—
Sad as his destiny!

VI.

Then I will sing
Of the daedal Earth

And the dancing stars;
The world shall ring
With the Titan's birth
And the deeds of Mars!

The glittering helm,
The quivering spear
And thrice bound shield;
Dark Pluto's realm,
With pale-faced Fear,
And hearts that yield!

I will sing of a spring,
And the 'wildering maze
Of its winding stream;
How the blue bells ring
When their heads they raise
'Neath the moon's soft beam!

How the light elves swing
On the bending blade
As it sways to the breeze;
And their wee songs ring
Thro' the gladsome glade
As they loll at ease!

They are borne to the sky—
To the infinite blue
And its archéd dome;
As they ride on high,
They are lost to view
In the spirit's home!

The fire-fly now
Suggesteth a song
As it wingeth the air;
With its radiant glow,
As it wendeth along,
And its meteor-glare!

As it wanders afar,
It is lost to the sight
In the measureless dark;
Like a full orbed star
It sprinkles the light
Of its luminous spark!

VII.

Why wilt thou grieve a heart forsworn?
  Already now the hour has past
  When melodies like thine may last;
Thy softest lay's received with scorn.

The wildest music Earth has given—
  The most irregular and sweet—
  Wherein the thought and action meet,
Were echoing symphonies of heaven.

  Then prythee, pipe a simple lay,
  Nor from the laws of metre stray;

The loveliest thought—the wildest throe;
The brightest joy—the deepest woe,
Will never once excuse the line
That breathes of sympathies divine!

VIII.

What! would'st thou bind the freedom of my verse?
By what old statute wouldest thou coerce?
Didst ever hear the thunder's distant roar,
Or the wild surges by the lone sea-shore?
Didst ever view the lights and shadows play
Upon the sleeping hills, and flee away
With lightning speed, until they cease to roam,
Vanquished and lost within the evening's gloom?
Then tell me in what ratio they move,
That I may learn of them to sing of love!

Each globe of night is tremulously hung
Self-poised in vacancy, and boundless space
Alone confines the ardor of the race,
As ray leads ray to mingle in the chase
To nothing tending, and from nothing sprung!

'Tis eve, and stillness reigns supreme!
Each wave of air speaks whisperingly low,
Lulling the spirit in its dream
Of voiceless happiness or saddening woe!
All pulseless is the heart; the noiseless flow
Of the pure Reason's limpid stream
Scarce wakes the burden of the outbreathed
    sigh;
The groves wherein the breezes lie,
Guarded of close-lipped Silence, anxious seem
To murmur Nature's holy lullaby:

IX.

The winds awake,
    The streamlets dance;

Grove nods to grove
    From its dreamy trance
And whispers, "love!"

The ruffled lake
    Inclines the ray;
From swell to swell
    The murmurs play,
And whisper, "well!"

The joyous birds
    Now swarm the moor;
A sweeter note
    Than e'er before
Now swells the throat.

The lark pours forth
    Her evening lay;
Like morning frost
    It melts away,
Forever lost!

Each thing of life's
  A happy 'wight;
Each supple wing
  Is bathed with light
Evanishing!

The free wind bends
  The scalloped boat;
Beneath the gale
  Two shadows float
With well trimmed sail!

X.

If thou would'st only ease my soul
  Of all that burns within it,
I'd praise thee with my latest breath;—
  Canst do it? Pray begin it.

Tell her—the maiden of my dreams—
  My heart still loves her dearly,

That every glance and every sigh
   Betokens how sincerely.

Tell her, I love her with a soul
   That feels it is a duty
To bend in reverence and awe
   Before the shrine of beauty;

That shame and scorn can never change
   The pure and constant spirit;
'Tis lost within the beautiful—
   'Twas formed to worship merit!

Oh! constancy's its own reward
   E'en tho' it may be slighted,
The flower it rears, the blossom love—
   Where didst thou find it blighted?

A gleam of hope expands its leaves,
   Tho' nipped within the hour,

Another and a lovelier bloom
    Bursts forth to prove its power!

The more you bend the fragrant tree
    The purer perfume sheds it,
Mild incense, mist-like, floats around,
    The air of heaven weds it!

XI.

Canst sing of love?—undying love?
    Canst paint a calm still yearning?
Canst whisper of the fiery tide
    Within the spirit burning?

    Canst murmur how
    I breathed a vow
To grace one shrine forever?
    Winged Time shall prove
    A spirit-love
No earthly tie may sever!

I'll do my best;
At thy behest
I'll paint the constant spirit;
I'll prove that love
Soars far above
High talent, mind, or merit!

Then pray begin,—
Thy guerdon win,—
Eternal fame elate thee;
The Graces stand
With wreaths in hand,
May bright success await thee!

Then be all ear;

Thou need'st not fear,
My spirit drinks each murmur;

List to a strain to ease thy pain
Then—cling to love the firmer!

XII.

I love a maid—I love but ane;
    She recks na of my love na me,
She binds me wi' a triple chain
    Whilst Joy sits laughing in her e'e!

Of faultless air, of matchless grace,
    She wiles my listless heart away
Each passing glory of her face
    Outrivals morn's serenest ray!

I love a maid—I love but ane;
    Soft music breathes from every feature,
Yet, whilst she gies all others pain
    God ne'er could mould a lovelier creature:

The sunny glance—the 'witching smile—
    The starlight tangled in her tresses
Which ever and anon the while
    Fall o'er her neck in soft caresses;

The snowy arm, its beauties bare,
    Beguiles my soul of all its leisure;
The floating meteor of her hair
    Has robbed my heart of every pleasure!

And whilst I sigh, and whilst I gaze,
    My burning spirit's hushed in sadness,
Lost far within the 'wildering maze
    Of deepening woe, and maniac gladness!

I love a maid—I love but ane;
    When God first breathed soft music o'er her
The flowers entrancéd of the strain
    With glowing bosoms bowed before her!

The wilding rose—her incense shed—
    Grew faint beneath excess of pleasure;
The poppy reared its dreamy head;
    The violet breathed its choicest treasure;

The blue bell tolled its fairy note—
    Tho' of its music ever chary,
The woodlark warbled from her throat—
    The dream of love—the name of Mary!

Ah, me! my heart! Thou, too, bewrayed
    Wert capturéd when all unwary,
The trembling note soft Nature made
    Breathed thro' thy chords the name of
        Mary!

The whisperings die—the accents faint—
    Yet still the rapture burns within me,
Whilst heart-throbs wed the voiceless plaint,
    Nae other murmur e'er shall win me!

Still will I love, and love but ane,
    Tho' naething save despair abide me,
Tho' madness seize upon the brain,
    And all who know me may deride me!

Still will I love, and love but ane,
   Tho' every freeborn thought forsake me,
And Fever with his ghastly train
   Of tort'ring phantasies, o'ertake me!

And when these lips are paled in death,
   Soft harmonies shall float between them—
The echoings of their former breath—
   Nae other strain shall e'er demean them!

The soul enraptured of that strain
   Around those lips shall restless hover,
Nae mair compressed with maddening pain
   But breathing of the constant lover!

And when laid low within the tomb,
   That voice shall wake the silent dust,
Earth's loathsome vault, and sombre gloom,
   Shall hold in vain the breathing bust!

The heart shall beat its measured stroke;
   Love's calm pulsations thrill the breast;
Till Death's stern power, forever broke,
   Leave conquering spirit to its rest!

ETERNITY.

Lost in a vision, I beheld, and lo!
An ocean—shoreless as the realms of night—
Toward which, as to a home, each restless
    wave
Points it froth-cap :—as tho' rest could be
    found
For that to which God whispers, "flow for-
    ever!"
No ebb was there—no tide; no beach whereon
To spread the dazzling white cloth of its foam;
For evermore, shoreless, surge strives with
    surge
To win a path straight forward to the goal
That still recedes before the combatants,
Enshrouded in the black pall of a night
Which knows no moon, nor solitary star

To unveil darkness in her drear retreat!
And then, oh, man! poor earthworm! reck-
     less fool!
I saw thee point the decorated prow
Wreathed with the painted baubles of the
     earth,
Toward that wild chaos of unending night,
As tho' ensured from shipwreck'd woe, and
     harm,
And life were but the plaything of the hour—
An evening sail upon an inland stream!

LINES ON FEELING.

When the golden tide of feeling
   Softly lulls the soul to rest,
A truer phase revealing
   Of the world within the breast,
'Tis then I love to wander
   'Mid the hills and painted fields,
Where pensive I may ponder
   The truths its ray reveals.

Far softer than the sunlight
   Upon a hazy day,
When the first bright beam of morniug
   Hastes to roll the mists away;
Far kindlier than the moonlight
   That dreams its life away

On the purple-tinted landscape
　　That is wearied of the day:

Far milder than the twilight
　　Which guards the gate of ev'n,
When the red orb seeks his rest,
　　And glooms the vault of heaven;
Far gentler than the starlight
　　That floods the darkened dome,
Is this golden tide of feeling
　　That calls the spirit home!

The soul—it often wanders
　　From its own ethereal sphere,
Life's truest wealth it squanders,
　　Nor counts its blessings dear;
It sighs for other pleasures
　　Than those true thought reveals;
It seeks for other treasures
　　Than those the spirit feels.

Oh! were it not for feeling,
   Heart might forever roam,
No voice to guide it rightly,
   No hand to point it home!
This steals upon the spirit
   Ere the soul be well aware,
In spite of each demerit
   It floats upon the air;

It softens every feeling,
   It soothes each care to rest,
And like a balm of healing
   Stills the tumults of the breast!
'Tis void of all impression,
   The soul could never give
Its faintest tints expression,
   Or bid its glories live!

        Thus,
When the golden tide of feeling

Softly lulls the soul to rest,
A truer phase revealing
  Of the world within the breast,
'Tis then I love to wander
  'Mid the hills and painted fields,
Where pensive I may ponder
  The truths its ray reveals!

THE UNIVERSAL HEART.

No soul so dark, or sunk so low,
But oft hath felt a nobler throe
Than e'er hath won a poet's name
Or twined the lasting crown of fame.

The wreaths they wear—the illustrious few—
They have derived from me and you;
Our common nature rears the flower
Their hands have plucked in kindlier hour.

With taste and care they weave and twine
The wreaths which should be yours and mine,
Then wear in cold insanity
The crown that's due humanity!

Tho' overflowing like the bowl
Of generous wine, the poet's soul

Is emptiness—inanity,
To the thoughts which bow humanity.

The universal heart shall beat
With deepening pulses, still and deep,
Tho' ne'er a dream that floods its mind
May spiritual expression find.

Its thoughts are deeper than the earth;
Thou, God, alone canst give them birth;
Toward thee alone still swells the tide
Engulfing all the world beside.

HYMN TO THE CATHOLIC CHURCH.

IN THE SPIRIT OF A CONVERT.

Had I but known thee, Church of God,
   Amid my boyish years,
I had not bowed beneath the rod
   Of servile hopes and fears:
Childish disciple at thy feet,
   I should have caught thine accents sweet
Nor wandered far from righteousness;
   Thou Spouse of Christ, our Saviour mild,
   Hadst hushed to calm the passions wild
Which rob me of my bliss!

Now that the midnight surges raise
   Their clamor to the sky,
Can Reason safely thread the maze
   Of strife and anarchy?

Alas! fair Reason's gaze is blind;
No other refuge may we find
Save thee, thou Church—thou ark of God!
   Hope as a rainbow gilds the storm;
   Fixed faith defends those hearts from harm
Whose trust is in his word!

I know that o'er the mountain's brow
   Thy chariot-wheels are heard!
I know the grieved and sorrowing now
   Are blessed within thy word!
To Thee I come, O Saviour mild,
A simple, trusting, tearful child—
Usher my spirit to thy rest;
   O lead me to thy Spouse on Earth;
   O bless me with the second birth
Low hushed upon thy breast!

Thou Spirit, point me to the path
   Of peace without alloy;

Ye holy martyrs shield from wrath
   A heart without a joy;
Be thine, sweet mother of my Lord,
The prayer which wins me to my God
And seals my soul from misery;
   A wretch, betrayed without, within,
   Sorely estranged by care and sin,
Dares raise his voice to Thee!

SONNET ON CHATTERTON.

ALREADY time has brought about the year,
Wherein I number days as fair and round
As those that youthful Chatterton have bound,
And ushered to death's gloom on boyhood's bier!
Would that my burning heart-throes were as dear
To man's warm pulse as his! That the sweet sound
Which speaks his praises, and points out the mound
Where genius lies, might lover-like be near
My sad remains! Oh! I would willingly
Be wrapped in slumber.'neath some flowery sod,
There to be hid, and there unconscious lie,
Till the dread trump should summon me to God,
Could that but win the love for which I burn,
And link my name to such as may not die!

DETERMINATION.

I DWELL in a whirl of ideas!
My fiery thoughts are the trampling steeds
That wing their way to the spheres!
Tramp! tramp! tramp!
How they beat the air with the burning hoof,
Rearing aloft, and roaring aloof,
Whilst my heart throbs wild with its fears!
Tramp! tramp! tramp!
With the aery step of Pegăsus,
Storming the pass to Parnassus!

In the fair morning dream of life,
The spirit wakens to inborn strength,
Gallantly arming for strife!
Strife! strife! strife!
Till Nature succumbs to the sturdy stroke
And her spirit-charms and chains are broke,

Which else would have bound us for life!
Strife! strife! strife!
With iron will and a constant aim:
Thus each spirit should dare a great fame!

THE HERMIT.

In a land of clustering roses, tinged with many a lively hue,
Where merry Sunshine braids her hair, and bares her breast to view;
In a land of lightsome echoes, sweeping wildly o'er the lyre
Soft Music hangs within the groves to wake and soothe desire,
Lived and died a lonely hermit, mild of eye and pure of heart—
For in shunning of the world's embrace he chose the nobler part—
When that Honor weaved a chaplet of fair hopes to grace his brow,
He had fled from earthly grandeur, binding on his soul, a vow.
With a spirit wed to Nature, in bright youth his soul had loved

Each living thing that breathed the air—each
 creeping thing that moved,
For his eye—it drank the glory of the amber-
 tinted sky,
And to his heart the wild winds spake that
 listless wandered by;
God had lulled him in the poet's dream, and
 with a poet's tongue
He pictured Earth as first she smiled, her
 pristine beauty sung;
He could paint the burnished mountains glowing in the evening's ray,
And o'er the blushing landscape make the
 rosy cloudlets stray.
When twilight-voices whisper, singing lullaby
 to Mirth,
And heavenly calm falls with the dew that
 glist'ning veils the Earth;
When Morning swings her censer thro' the
 dreamy realms of air,

In lowliness of spirit, see him kneel and offer
    prayer:
Thus mysteries are lightened, and his soul
    is lost in day,
Whilst angel forms, with shining spears,
    thrust Darkness far away,
The future—sweetly smiling on the present—
    points above
To glorious clouds of witnesses which throng
    the throne of Love.

MORAL.

Thus in Age the heart is gladdened, and on
    angel-wings shall soar
When scattered locks and feeble steps pro-
    claim the conflict o'er;
For the soul that shunneth evil in the early
    morn of Youth,
E'en in Time shall view Eternity, and wear
    the crown of Truth!

SONG.

Who loves not to gaze
   On the timid-eyed gazelle,
As she wanders 'mid the maze
   Of the hills she loves so well?
By the crystal fount that flows
   Murmuring, murmuring
Joy to the breezy groves,
   Answering, answering,
Gaily she trips along,
Keeping step to Nature's song!

But I love more to gaze
   Into woman's gentle eye,
As her lashes soft are raised
   In rapture to the sky,
For I feel, and I know
   There's more music in her soul,
Than unseen choirs in wandering
   In spirit-measures roll!

LINES TO MISS R. L. N.

With a smile of sunshine,
   With an eye of laughter
Driving on their merry dance
Tripping sunbeams; with a glance
Such as sparkles warm with wine,
   Or the dream—hereafter :

With a soul, displaying
   Treasuries of beauty
Ever riveting the gaze;
Overflowing with the praise
It would fain be saying
   In defence of duty :

With the hope of heaven
   'Graven on thy spirit;—
As thou art, we love thee,
With the dreams which move thee,
For to such is given
   More than worldly merit!

SONNET

On the erection of Bartholomew's Statue of Washington over the store of N. W., of Baltimore, January 23d, 1859.

WHO would have thought it, mighty Washington,
That form as sacred to each heart as thine,
Tho' lifeless marble; e'er would be a sign
To marshal in "the trade?" And Thou! Great Son!
America's lost Joy—whose race has run—
Thrice mourned Bartholomew! Had'st Thou forseen
This horrid sacrilege of things divine,
The cold, cold lips of stone had wreathed their scorn

'Neath thy creating hand! Then thou, in
    tears
Repentant, streaming in a hallowed flood
Adown thy careworn cheeks, had poured thy
    blood
Christening Earth, rather than future years,
Pure guardians of thy miracles and name,
Should scar thy scutcheon with a soiléd fame!

SONNET.

*To Mrs. Fanny Kemble, upon hearing her
read Macbeth, December 20, 1858.*

INIMITABLE actress of the soul,
The languages of Reason and the Heart,
Woven adroitly in each subtle part,
When thou art reading, on the senses roll!
That voice alone could well express the whole
Had not thine eye its meanings to impart!
Now hushed to calm we sit, and now we start!
Each will dethronéd, yields its weak control
Over passionate desires unto thee,
That thou mayest train them in obedience
To fickle government, till they shall see
Vain opposition ends in impotence,
Without a show of reason or of sense,
While to submit is truly to be free!

LINES.

My heart expanded like a flower
    Too early blown,
Uncherished by mild April-shower,
    Or rearing sun.

Where it lies withered, others wave
    In crimson dress;
Their leaves the dripping night-dews lave—
    Soft winds caress.

What tho' they dance and sing aloud—
    All, all must die!
The sparkling dew shall glide, a shroud
    From noiseless sky.

The summer drops which sank in showers,
    Soon wintry frost,

With biting tongue will nip the flowers,
    Their beauty lost.

Thus hearts awaken at a sigh
    To thrills of love,
And by that glance are doomed to die,
    In which they throve!

Where, where on earth, poor fleeting one,
    Can longing find—
Or lingers there beneath yon sun—
    A steadfast mind?

Say—is love's ecstasy a balm,
    And to be given
That heart alone, which spirit-calm
    Unfolds in heaven?

Alas! that God's discerning lot
    Should call so few,

And myriad souls should die for what
    They never knew!

My heart, clasp thou the Infinite!
    Thy treasure find
Thro' approbation in his sight—
    The purest kind!

Earth's jewels flash the gaudy ray,
    An hour's joy;
The diamond's lustre wells from clay,
    A base alloy.

Seek thou for truths immutable
    As God's own throne;
Feel thou that joys of spirit well
    From God alone.

TO LILI DURING HER ABSENCE.

The beautiful, they pine for thee
   When thou art far away,
They yearn to bask in thy sweet smile,
   They whisper, " dinna stay!"

The flowerets—the rivulets—
   The glades and sunny meads,
Are languishing for thy sweet smile—
   The passion flower bleeds.

The stars in silence guard the night
   And mark each fleeting hour,
The sun reels darkling on his flight—
   The threatening dun clouds lower.

Each heart which loves the beautiful,
   Now thou art far away,

Shall throb in holy unison—
 "Ah, Lili! dinna stay!"

Ah! could'st thou hear the earnest prayer
 All Nature breathes for thee,
A joyous tear—a maiden's tear
 Would tremble in thine e'e.

'Twould wound thy tender soul to think
 That thou wast far away;
Thou would'st not have it in thine heart,
 To make a longer stay.

There is a heart—a poor lone heart—
 It bleeds each lengthened day,
'Tis lost within the beautiful—
 It whispers, "dinna stay!"

It looks to thee—it beats for thee,
 Thou measurest every stroke,

Thou art its pulse, and shall be so
  Until each chord be broke.

Thou art its dream—its heaven-born dream;
  Thou art its every sigh;
Thou art the spirit of the thrill
  When none save God is nigh.

Thou art the fervor of its power;
  Thou art its quiet calm;
Thou art the tumult of its throes;
  Thou art its holiest balm:

And still it mourns, and still it sighs
  That thou art far away;
Each warm pulse notes the fleeting hour
  And whispers, " dinna stay!"

The beautiful, they yearn for thee;
  They pine to view thy grace;

They're languishing for thy sweet smile—
    They long to see thy face : . .

And thus they swell the saddening plaint,
    " Ah, Lili, dinna stay !
The true—the pure—they canna thrive
    When thou art far away !"

LINES TO MISS S. W——.

Could gentle thoughts, and modest worth,
Win crowns and diadems of earth,
The fairest and the most serene
Should bind thy brow, mild Nature's Queen.

In haughty state, let Fashion wear
Rich clustering jewels in her hair,
No mine of Ind could e'er impart
A joy like to thy joy of heart.

As when the silvery cloud at ev'n
Is rather to be felt than seen,
So lost within the amber sky
That either claims the brilliancy;

The thrills which thou awak'st in me,
Tho' warm with life, are lost in thee,
Till each dear rapture makes me feel
How every dream I have, I steal!

THE LITTLE CLOUD.

'Tis twilight's quiet, and the far off sky
Is softly pencilléd of amber hue,
As tho' an artist had employed his skill
In shade and sunlight thro' refraction's
    power;
Proving that Nature needeth not the shroud
Of darkness edged with gold, in the black
    woof
Which ofttimes veils the smiling face of
    heaven—
Thinking to add new grandeur to a scene
Resplendent with mild graduated shades
Of high wrought coloring, and well thrown
    light!
Let the eye glance in strictest scrutiny
From west to north, and thence unto the east

Until it sweep the whole horizon's rim,
And rests its wearied ray, where in the south
A silver clasp weds joyous Earth to Heaven,
And not a single covert can be found,
Wherein the bright idea, speaking to man
In colors tremulous, and deathless tints,
From every quarter of the firmament,
Could well conceal its radiance from the gaze.

And yet, behold! *There* is a little cloud,—
Not larger than a hand,—of crescent shape,—
With edges wavy and irregular,
Of which the body is so shadowy
That the bold eye can pierce midway the veil
Which robs it of a single span of blue!
It seems as tho' God's providence directs
Its every motion through the azure vault,
So slowly floats it, that the doubt might rise
Whether it move at all, save that the thought
Of Nature's ministry in use of things—

Prime law, immutable, ordained of God—
Gives life and action to minutest forms.

Reclined beside a stream of musical voice,
Carving a loved one's name upon the bark
Of the sad cypress tree—as tho' that name
Were wed to sadness, and a spirit, warmed
With deepest fervor, and wild rhapsody
Of love unchangeable that outlives life—
Entwined within the free strings of the heart—
Whose lyre is swept alone of passion's hand—
Most like enwoven harmony of verse,
And Music's deeper soul of untaught strains—·
And lost in musing on this very point
Of God's eternal providence, displayed
In agency and use of Nature's power
Innate, and self-applied, I often glance
Upward with calm delight, to note the change
That, shadowlike, steals o'er the face of
    things—

A spirit-veil—enhancing loveliness
Thro' the mild softening of sky-scenery.

But see! the sky alone receives not all
The mild reflection; for the little cloud
Which heretofore seemed uselessly to rob
The roving vision of its form of blue,
Receives one trembling ray upon its breast,
Softening, and softening thro' diffusive power,
Until it greets the glad eye with a smile
Like to the waving amber-shafted wheat
Ripe unto the sickle, when that a storm
Bathes the warm brow of Earth, in passing
    showers
Of cooling rain, and sunlight plays between,
Wild gambols with the streams, and woods,
    and flowers!
Already, as tho' conscious of the power
Of adding grace, and elegance, and ease,
To Nature's mild repose from weariness—

Now that the mantling shades invite to rest—
It grows in beauty like a flower in bloom!
The little cloud has changed into the moon,
And that which hid a single span of blue,
Now lights, irradiates, and chastens all!

Hail! Queen of Night! and mistress of my
    heart!
Thy smile is like the ray of inward peace
Lighting the deep recesses of a soul
Lost far within the beautiful—and God!

LINES TO MISS G. C——.

Youth weaves a crown for later years,
Of glowing hopes, and pallid fears,
    Then pines to see
The opening blush of many a flower,
Which closed, awaits the full-blown hour
    To burst it free.

Alas! tho' many bloom full fair,
Yielding sweet incense to the air,
    Some few I ween
Are paled by stern reality—
The sorrows of humanity
    Too often seen.

The crown thus varied, binds the brow
Of all who know or love us now;
    'Tis but too true

Fond Hope can never bloom alone !
Pale—marble-pale—as carved from stone
      Springs Sorrow too !

Twin sisters dear ! I would not part
That sisterhood, or ease the heart
      Of one sad care;
This, bids Earth's brightest colors shine !
That, whispers softly, " Heaven is thine—
      Hence ! dark Despair !"

Oh, may thy youthful spirit weave
A crown, whose radiance mild may leave
      No shade behind—
Chaplet of innocence and worth,
The rainbow clasp of Heaven and Earth—
      A tranquil mind !

SONNETS TO CONSTANCE.

I.

For three long weeks I've pined to see thee,
    Constance!
Now that fond hope must yield unto despair,
I have bethought me of my God and prayer,
And penned these lines, alas! a vain remon-
    strance!
What pleasure canst thou find in such a dance
As thou hast led me? Lovers and loved ones
    stare
Wonderingly on thee! First, thy beauty rare
Rivets each joy-sick sense, turning the glance
Of thousands upon one: which thou repayest
By all the myriad pretty things thou sayest
With every speaking feature! Then they ask
Inquiringly about thee, and a heart

As yet unmoved save by the forms of Art,
And who aspire within thy smile to bask;

II.

Whilst I, forsaken of my own sweet hope,
Must 'minister the short-lived joy to such,
As seeing thee, already love too much!
Feebly essaying with a god to cope,
Smitten with blindness, how they reel and grope
Feeling for light! And if perchance they touch
One chord of sympathy or feeling in thee,
Awakening a rapture in that breast
Which heretofore lay slumbering, oh! how blest
The ecstasy which thrills them, henceforth free!

But should thy gentler thought be veiled
 from them—
And they may fail to read thy soul aright—
No soothing voice of Music, no fair dream
Of what might be, can heal the heart's sad
 blight!

LINES.

IN THE SPIRIT OF UNIVERSALISM.

When racked upon the bed of pain
   Delirious thought would scan,
Visions, that ne'er might rise again,
   Of life in Nature—man;
No fear of dissolution fell
Upon the soul; no dread of hell
   Could blear those phantasies of mind!
Where'er the active spirit soared,
Tho' lightnings flashed, and thunders roared,
   'Twas peace for human kind!

Thanks, glorious Being! for the theme
   Which thus engaged my song;
Great God! and was it all a dream—
   And is Thy teaching wrong!

Ye happy few who hold the truth
Impressed upon the soul in youth
   By laughing meads of Earth and sky,
Go! In your joy spread far and wide
That misery Soul shall ne'er betide,
   Nor anguish wake her sigh!

Fair Nature wields no threatening rod
   About our lowly head;
Each roseate blush—a prayer to God—
   Still bids us love—not dread!
No pang attends the violet's death,
Into the air she yields her breath
   The mildest effluence of the hour;
And while these emblems prove his care
Embracing ocean, earth, and air,
   Creation speaks his power!

Great God! how do I see and praise
   Each wondrous act above!

A Prince art Thou in all thy ways—
   A fount of guileless love!
Nor faithless I—but faithless they
Who would thy character bewray,
   And stamp thy work an infamy!—
These dastard hearts, which ceaseless break
Thy laws, shall of those mercies take
   They would deny to me!

LINES.

Fair Lili's heart's the tent of Love,
With threads of feeling interwove;

Joy's laughing fountain wells within—
Oh! who would not the curtains move!

Steal gently—the rich damask draw—
And thus my bold assertion prove!

How fortunate, whoe'er may view
There pillowéd, a rosy Love!

Could others see what I have seen
Oh! who would not my choice approve!

TO AMORET.

In burning verse, or learning's lore,
   Could I but meet as mild a thought
   As thy sweet smile from Nature caught,
'Twould fill my heart—I'd need no more!

But having once on Beauty gazed
   The soul would loiter at her shrine;
   Yet, now thy love may ne'er be mine
I must confess the siege is raised!

Since prayer is wind, and useless sighs
   But wake a tumult hard to bear,
   I will no longer sit and stare,
Or drown my soul in thy deep eyes!

I'll say I ne'er did love their light;
   Tho' I have pined the livelong day

    To catch the shadow of a ray
Which round them ran its circlets bright!

And when their sunlets flashed but scorn,
    I've bowed my soul in humbleness,
    Which witnessèd the heart's distress
That e'er such hapless wight were born!

But when in liquid tenderness
    Their rays might pour a flood of grace—
    E'en hallowing another's face—
Oh! I could scarce my joy repress!

My soul is like the swelling tide—
    The heavy—restless—surging sea;
    The moon's full glories like to thee,
Which peacefully its billows ride!

I toss with longings like the sea;
    But never may the surges rise
    To wed that glory of the skies—
So I may never wed with thee!

THE DEAD.

Sweet is thy liquid voice, O bell,
    To the dead!
Soothing the air on whose pinions it floats
    Far, far away,—
    Thro' the realms of day,—
As the sunbeam dances, jeweled with motes;
Sweetest and wildest of melodies
To the dead! To the dead!

And fair thy flower-wreathed brow, O Earth!
    To the dead!
Low hushed is the pulse to list to the toll
    Of spirit-bells,
    With whose laughter, wells
Mild Music's earnest and tearful soul;

Waking her harmonies morning and eve,
For the dead! For the dead!

Deepest and purest of Earth, is the dream
      Of the dead!
O'er life's dull languor it floats like a crown
      Star-'cintured, and gleaming
      With radiance; seeming
To sink with the shadowy air, gliding down
From regions of spirit, an angel-crown
From the dead! From the dead!

LINES

COMPOSED AFTER AN ILLNESS.

Into the world unknown,
By mad delirium thrown
'Mid changing states, and loftier flights of brain,
Entranced, how Being reeled!
Life's conscious fount unsealed,
Renewed in mind the fear of deepening pain:
Then—not till then—could Truth assert her sway
O'er dreaming Will, which slept from day to day!

Intensity of thought
A drearier sense has wrought
Of hourly anguish traced in lines of care;

Life is not all a dream,
As sluggish spirits deem,
There's time for mirth—now death invites to
    prayer :
My God! restore pure childhood's trustful
    love ;
Be Thou my guide where'er I erring rove !

Can man renew the heart ?
Can sated sense impart
Beauties primeval—joys of pristine source ?
Thou, Saviour mild, alone,
From sympathetic throne
Canst re-create—derive a gain from loss ;
Inspire the trembling hope of pardoning grace ;
The heart that loves, shall see Thee face to
    face !

Can hypocritic cant
Supply a spirit-want ?—

Low in Earth's pageant let us bow the knee!—
    What! what if reason fail
    Whilst fiendish hosts prevail?
Let Will regenerate climb the heights to Thee!
Pressed heart to heart, Earth's favored sons
    repose,
Reclaimed from sin, protected from their foes!

    How can a soul unsaved,
    'Mid myriad hosts enslaved,
Gain pure delights— ecstatic thrills of heaven?
    A panacea yield
    For such as keep the field,
May angels whisper—"hark, their sin's for-
    given!"
Immortals! never weary of the strife!
To fail—is death! To win—eternal life!

LINES.

RESPECTFULLY DEDICATED TO OUR HOUSE OF REPRESENTATIVES.

Ye gods! To think that Jove allows such strife
Of hearts and tongues, to mar poor human life!
Such combinations of pretence and power;
Such threatening clouds of nothingness to lower!
Was gift of gab but given us of God
To prove that men, as well as logs, are bored?
When monarchs tremble for their wide domains,
And civil broils enhance war's grievous pains;
When rival squadrons flout the oppresséd sea
With flying streamers and artillery,

And safety hangs upon the sure command
Of those empowered to bid them flee, or stand;
Then, little instrument, thy voice is heard,
For pending interests hang upon a word :
Then God commands thee speak, for weal or
    woe ;—
But *this*—is waging war without a foe!

Tell, mighty wag! Say, rattling clap-trap,
    say!
What guides thy pendulum's mysterious
    sway?
Why works one word an hundred thousand
    fold
More than ten times the number useless
    rolled?
The cause alone gives weight unto the wind—
For words are nothing more than puffs of
    mind!

Come! Sit and listen to this wild debate
Of mingled nonsense—charity?—and hate!—
How the eye sparkles when some dodge is found
To gain the floor, and pour the useless sound;
See the fat hand extended towards the roof—
As tho' dumb Nature was not nonsense proof:—
Whilst every eye is strained, and every ear,
To catch the sentiment they like or fear;
How men are swayed as tho' by clock-work's power
Be thy revealment, O thou future hour!
What ranting—tearing, of both mind and head—
Such wholesale butchery of whate'er was said
Ere that the learned member gained the floor,
Was never seen or ever heard before!
What sharp presentiment of coming strife—

Of principles already formed, and rife
Within the magic-weaving, muddling brain
Of Mr. ——, who, getting floor again,
Will perchance argue points just so, and so,—
Amend the motion by a well aimed blow
Of policy farsighted—straight aware
That such a dodge will make opponents stare :
Great Jove! What would the heavenly coun-
    cils say,
To hear, de facto, such men dare to pray!
And yet they beat and bang at heaven's door,
E'en whilst misusing, praying hard for more!
Oh! may they, Twist-like, stretch the empty
    bowl,
Poor, brainless pates, mean starvelings of
    soul!

TO MISS N. S.

I KNEW a timid child,
   A gentle, winning maiden;
No dreams her heart beguiled,
   Save such as sweetly laden
With perfumes of the Heaven and Earth,
Were symbols of her beauteous birth!

Where'er the wild Winds bend
   The crimson-tippéd flowers,
Thither her lone steps tend
   To while away the hours;
The beauties of her mind expand
With every blush that paints the land!

The glories which surround
   Her form, are varied beauties;
An union here is found,

TO MISS N. S.

Of pleasing traits and duties—
Deep sympathies with human kind,
Of heart and hand, of soul and mind!

Light, shadow-like, attends
   Her steps where'er they wander;
The star of evening bends
   Her loveliness to ponder,
Hoping at some far distant day
Its orb may yield as mild a ray!

THE DEATH BED.

A young man being desperately ill, and acquainted with his near dissolution, requested a young lady to be sent for; they were friends, nothing more. On the approach of death, he asked her to kiss him, with which request the lovely young girl complied. The following lines are respectfully dedicated to one in every way an honor to her sex.

BLESSED be the heart,
Which forth from out its urn of feeling, poured
A bright and genial flood
To cool that fevered brow!

Cheering the gloom,
Gathering in darkness o'er a wintry sky,
When nameless dread drew nigh—
An angel-form she stood!

When from thin lips,
Pallid, and bloodless as the sifted snow,
The soul's wild longings flow,
They plead—nor plead in vain!

Those earnest orbs
Soon to be closed in an eternal night,
Tho' paling now their light,
A faint thanksgiving yield!

The poet's theme!
May she survive to grace the willing song,
Its warmest sigh prolong,
Heart-burdened with her praise!

NATURE'S VOICE.

How musical the voice that wakes the dells
At early morn, ere that the merry hounds,
And jocund train which wait Aurora's blush,
Rouse slumbering Echo from her placid rest,
And envious sun-beams ramble thro' the meads,
Sipping the pendent orbs of purest light
All trembling with love-zeal—courting the glance
Which drains them of their beauty, and their Being!
'Tis hard to think it of a world so vast,
Yet truth still calls for truth; the great round Sun—
The eye of God—most beautifully bright,
Which meets no rival in his lordly path

And drinks the timid starlight at a draught—
Which, all the livelong night, with silvery
    veil
Woven of fairy sprites on Nature's loom,
Conceals betrothéd Earth from lawless gaze—
Is moved to jealousy by drops of light
That grace and bathe her brow: lest her fond
    heart
That ever loved the fair and beautiful,
Be won of delicacy more than power!

Let envy cease! Cease vain solicitude!
She prides her that her heart of hearts is
    thine;
And, lest she lose thy soul-inspiring glance,
She throws aside the drapery of the hour
With which she tawdily bedecked herself,
To while away the "lazy-pacing" points
Called seconds in the reckoning of time,

Which go to join th' immeasurable past,
And herald thy return! It is her wish
To meet thee, robed in pure simplicity,
Winning thee to herself thro' natural charms,
Such as first won thy mild approving gaze
When the great God bequeathed her to thy
  care,
And bade thee cherish her, till Death and Woe
Should swallow up all forms which dream of
  life,
And Chaos once again ascend his throne
Of ebon darkness, 'mid the crash of sphere
Hurled against sphere, reeling to accomplish
A direful fate and final destiny.
Thou wouldst not rob her of the modest
  flowers
For them thou gavest her; and as thy gift
She prizes them beyond the crystal dew
That she dispenses with at thy approach;

And when thou comest thro' the eastern gate,
She welcomes thee in silence, and with smiles
That are reflections of thine own sweet gaze!
The drowsy air, aroused from listlessness—
Her swift-soled messenger—she sends to thee,
Deep-laden with the perfume of the flowers
Which cluster round her palpitating heart!
And she would fain breathe forth a prayer to
    thee,
Piercing the dark-ribbed clouds, which inter-
    cept
The golden shower of thy laughing beams,
Were not her mild voice hushed in man's sad
    fall!

God, in creating, smiled upon his work,
And forthwith Earth possessed of conscious-
    ness—
For in the smile of God dwells Life, whilst
    Death

Swift-pinioned, drops attendant on his frown—
Preferred a prayer to Him for reason high,
Wed to a voice well trained in utterance
Of burning thought, and spirit-ecstasies:
He, answering hope by its accomplishment,
Gave infant man unto her nursing arms,
And bade her train him in true utterance
Of mysteries; thus she would be relieved
Of untold fires which waste her dreamy breast.
Him thus she would have reared, and oft she
    strove
To win him to herself, swaying his heart
Thro' the eternal union of soft love
With whatsoe'er is beautiful to mind;
Thus, by allurements, did she hope to
    guide
His fickle intellect to sterner laws
Of Being absolute—dependent forms:
Striving to raise a question in his thoughts
Of how the creature springs to life and sense

From the mere fiat of creative Will.
But he as oft took cognizance of sense,
O'erlooked the grandeur of eternal truths,
In mild reflections on the fires, which flare
Like lamps, beneath the wind-swept canopy
Of heaven's emblazoned roof; the moon—the stars,
Entranced his eyes by night—his Soul by day,
Lighting the world of mind with spirit-rays!

Yea, often, too, when wandering thro' the glades,
Young buds in coyness raised their lowly heads,
Blushing in maiden modesty, to win
His manly gaze; and then have drooped for shame,
That tints as gentle and as mild as theirs

Ne'er won remark, e'en in his kindlier hours!
Alas! that it is so! Had man but known
What eloquence there slumbered, unex-
    pressed,
Dependent on his rhapsodies of mind
Fair Earth could well inspire, but not direct;
His whole attention, concentrated where
The noblest principles can be evolved
By stern reflection, soon would have disclosed
The hidden glories of both mind and form;
Such joyful symphony from thence had
    sprung,
His foster mother ne'er had mourned a voice
As musical as that which guides the spheres,
Thro' all the mazes of the giddy dance
Sweeping the vast infinitude of space!

BALLAD.

WITH lily-white hand on her bosom of snow
To musical symphonies moving, as though
   Soft playing the strings of her heart,
Sits Maggie! Sky glitters above, whilst below,
Earth, floating in charms that mellifluous flow
From sympathy's spring, hangs bathed in the glow
   Fair Nature alone may impart.

Her eye were too warm, save to mellow its ray—
   Like pencil of evening subduing the day—
The spirit that thrills in her breast,
Drains inward the stream of the light, which denied

The throng of her lovers, is poured in a tide
Of dazzling soul-beams, disarming the pride
  Of strangers, and foes to her rest.

Ah! many have drooped for a glance of her
    eye;
And many, sore wounded, have left—with a
    sigh—
  Fair Maggie, when waking her heart:
That glance is to slay—that lily-white hand
None clasp save in friendship, for such her
    command:
Tho' suitors have offered what few can with-
    stand,
  Love-baffled is love's every dart.

Far away! Far away! in the clime of the South
Where bright stars sprinkle rays on the gor-
    geous Earth
  And songs ever gladden the hour,

Roams the youth of her choice: that youth,
   who alone—
Far away tho' he be—can awaken the tone
Of affection, soft welling from lyre of stone,
   As incense exhales from a flower.

TO THE EXILES OF ITALY.

Exiles from a bleeding land—
 Welcome! Welcome!
Tho' no jostling crowds be nigh
When the bright keels kiss the strand,
 Myriad-hosts should raise the cry:
  "Welcome! Welcome!"
Waving flags of liberty—
Shouting—" Hail the victor-band!
 Welcome! Welcome!"

Have ye failed, ye steadfast few?
 Never! Never!
Ne'er a blow is struck in vain!
Once our fathers bled like you!
 Life-drops rust oppression's chain
  Ever! Ever!

Gallant hearts will share your pain!
Tyrants shall this welcome rue,
    Ever! Ever!

God bless bleeding Italy
    Ever! Ever!
  When we grasp her fevered hand,
Nations! hearken to her sigh!
  Noble souls! our homes command
    Ever! Ever!
Can we an appeal withstand
In behalf of liberty?
    Never! Never!

LINES ON UNFORTUNATE LOVE.

I loved too young!
My eyes revealed my pain—
Alas! alas! in vain—
   Before my tongue!

Still shall they rove!
My heart by impulse swayed,
Ne'er, ne'er shall be allayed,
   Save thro' sweet love!

Deepens my thought!
Confined within a breast
That knows no joy nor rest,
   Tho' hourly sought!

Could beauty ease,
Here are an hundred eyes

LINES ON UNFORTUNATE LOVE. 171

That sprinkle love with sighs,
   Whispering—" Cease,

" Cease wandering free!
Where spirit-waters gush,
There let weak'ning passion hush
   Its boisterous sea!"

When laid in calm,
May Will her vigils keep
O'er demons, lulled to sleep
   In slumber's balm!

Health's rosy glow
Upon a dimpled cheek—
Is't this which thou dost seek
   My soul? Ah, no!

A kindred heart?
Yes! yes! I mark it well,

For thee, there is a hell
    Deep-hewn, apart!

Others can choose
A brighter, lovelier dream,
And in another's theme
    Their sorrows lose!

Sad is his fate,
Whom loving maids despise!
Who wakens tears with sighs
    To win but hate!

LINES ON GENIUS.

DEDICATED TO DR. C. J.

   How thankful he should be,
   Whoe'er hath chanced to see
A genius rear the god within his breast;
   Who viewed the raging fire
   Of uncontrolled desire
To act high deeds, invade a spirit-rest!
   When by a great thought tossed,
   All consciousness is lost
Of sun, and moon, and stars—of death and life,
   Rapt fairy-realms of soul
   His every sense control,
Till wearied Will again renews the strife;
Who living, but would willingly give o'er
His fairest dream, and with that spirit soar!

Spontaneous thrills of heart,
Serenest thoughts impart,
As sparkling crests ride waves of softest light;
Reason supreme attends,
And when commanded, bends,
Moulding to beauty, forms which blind the sight.
Thus from the realms of nought,
Mild shapes are hourly brought,
Whilst varied raptures fair, enchant the view;
Mind riveted to mind,
Heart's greatest wealth shall find,
In probing Nature for the bright and true!
May genius, as its works, for aye endure,
That man may cherish still, the chaste and pure!

TO AMORET.

Say, lovely maiden, say!
   Why flee the light?
Mild charms should woo the day;
   Few are so bright:
Cupid, in golden chains,
Prays thee to ease his pains!

Dost yet in freedom hold
   Maidenly thought?
Fear, lest that over bold,
   Thou mayest be brought—
Proud tho' thou be—so low
All may deride thy woe!

Hearts lost and won on Earth,
   Oft lose their power,
Waked to a nobler birth

Love rules the hour;
Fear, lest unknown to thee
Thy heart may vanquished be!

Shouldst thou refuse my prayer—
   Still hear my sigh;
When hope dissolves in air
   Sorrow is nigh;
Oh! soothe the galling pain,
E'en whilst you forge the chain!

Waft back the dreams of youth—
   Recall the hour
Light sighs were wed to truth
   Thro' Beauty's power:
Then, weave in, fair and free,
Visions and dreams of thee!

Thus tho' my heart may mourn
   Laden with sorrow,
New dreams shall bid me turn

Hope to the morrow:
E'en pain will rapture prove,
When wed to those we love!

TO MIRIAM.

I know thee, lovely Miriam, what thou art—
A cold, insensate form, without a heart!

The moon-beam loves to nestle in thy hair;
The fainting Zephyrs whisper, thou art fair:—

Yet Earth is all too warm a home for thee:
Thou canst not feel the throbbing of the sea!

The delicate tendrils, as they branching twine
Around the oak, suggest no love divine!

The joyous smile which lights the fields of air,
Speaks not of God, nor whispers he is there!

When thro' thy lattice, laughing Morn would take
A peep at thee, and thy soft slumbers break;

Aurora blushes that she must behold
Such breathless beauty cast in icy mould!

Oh! learn to view the hand of God, endued
With matchless power to work thee harm or
 good;

A power displayed in myriad worlds, up hung
In boundless space, fair on their centres
 swung;

A mind applied to form the insect's wing;
A hand that mingles odors of the Spring!

And if thou wouldst a living joy impart,
Pray God to gift thee with a human heart:

Thus mayest thou Yearn, how love is holier still
Than heartless beauty, paining by its thrill!

AN ADDRESS TO MY IMPULSE.

WILT thou ne'er prove false to me
Heart-awakened melody?
Thro' the dim revolving years
Thickly strewn with hopes and fears,
Wilt thou still remain by me
Heart-awakened melody?

Ah! I feel, when youth is past,
And the brow is overcast,
Blackened with the blows of life
Driven in amid the strife,
Thou—with other friends—shalt flee,
Heart-awakened melody!
Yet, tho' then my soul shall bow,
I will glory in thee now!

Tell me—if 'tis given to tell—
Whence pure springs of rapture well?

Mellows love in woman's voice,
Or the gentle, rustling noise
When the Zephyr longing breathes
Thro' myriad-hosts of leaves!
Whisper of the purple West,
And the landscapes crowned with rest!
Tell me—if 'tis given to tell
Whence pure springs of rapture well—
Why thou comest like a sigh
Forced to wander listlessly?
Why thou dost to pleasure wake
Hearts thou leavest soon to break?
Whether Love or Poesy
Is the name most dear to thee!
I would know thee, what thou art,
For I feel thou rul'st my heart!

Art thou Thought—or art thou Feeling?
Art thou but a ray, revealing

Hidden jewels of the mind,
Thought without thee ne'er could find?

Art thou Intuition's self?
Or a prank of that wild elf,
Whispering to ingenuous souls :
" Here the tide of treason rolls,
Hidden deep in dastard breast,
Which forever lost to rest,
Hates to view the sacred peace
Of another soul at ease!"
Tell me, for thou rul'st my heart—
I would know thee as thou art?

Tho' thou wert a misery—
Tho' thou wert an open lie
Given to this end—deceiving
All who must go on believing,
Whilst thou pourest out thy sigh
On the spirit, seemingly

AN ADDRESS TO MY IMPULSE.

Urging to a noble end;
Tho' I knew thee for a fiend—
Yet my spirit loves thee so
I'd thy every bidding do!

Is the culture of the heart
Madness? Dost thou e'er impart
Glories of the soul, to those
Who are idiots from repose?

Tell me! Is this restlessness
But the shadow of the bliss,
Spirit-calm, and rest of heaven,
To the sainted heroes given—
Such as, 'mid the battle's din,
Warred for God, and vanquished sin?

Yet, and if thou answerest not
These, the questionings of heart,
May thy sweet tones whisper me
Thro' a love-eternity!

AMBITION.

It is a sad, disheart'ning lot,
    To feel that other minds can soar
To airy heights, which we dare not
    Attempt to clamber o'er!

That brethren and companions dear,
    Tho' bound to us by social ties,
Will not by our suggestions steer
    Their courses for the skies!

Ambitious souls which feel the weight
    Of glory every mind can bear,
Are even fain to underrate
    The genius that they fear!

When cured of envy's sting, the heart
    Is guided of pure love again,
Time—time alone, will heal that smart
    Which pierces every vein!

AMBITION.

Let each true man contentment find,
    In that he bears an image bright,
Stamped lastingly upon the mind,
    And traced in living light!

Great hearts are but weak tools within
    The iron grasp of Nature's Lord,
And when reclaimed from pride and sin,
    Yield praise alone to God!

No honor claim they as their due;
    No thought original; no way
Can they point out as sure and true,
    To lead men to the day!

Less honored souls should e'en rejoice
    That God can sometimes use frail man—
A clarion to resound his voice—
    And tell us all He can!

AMELIA.

A FRAGMENT.

The following lines are fragmentary—connected only by the Author's private knowledge of plan, and future development. Fearing lest his little book—from want of patronage—may be the only one he will be enabled to give to the world, he thinks it appropriate to publish in this crude form that, which at some future date may possibly take a more decided mould and character.

FAIR is the smile of the Earth, for Morning has sprinkled the sunshine
Veiled in the globules of rain that noiselessly dripped from the heavens,
Far over meadow and lea, bathing the landscape in glory!
Long white peninsular clouds lose their capes in the still blue water
Arched far above—a measureless sea—an ocean of laughter!

Fair is the smile of the Earth, tho' Evening had witnessed the gray mists
Cover the deep-souled sky as the foam hangs over the billows,
Mingling shadowy forms—scattering the spray of the snow-flakes
Melting for love of the first warm kiss Earth gave them as greeting!
Warm is the smile of the Earth, but milder the glance of Amelia
Plays o'er the fair-haired boy she leads by the hand to the cottage,
Softly uplifting the latch which fastened the door of their dwelling,
As tho' afraid of disturbing the rest which had fallen from heaven—
Slumber of peace—on the tremulous limbs of her blind old father.
Gently they pass thro' the door—the boy and the maiden together;

Nearer and nearer they glide towards the
    chair with the tread of a shadow,
Kissing the floor of the room—their feet—
    with as noiseless a blessing.
Wed to the sorrows of age, the music of
    youth's deathless longings
'Wilders the old man's brain,—as the wind
    sweeps over the wind harp
Swung midway from a branch of a tree 'twixt
    Earth and the Heavens—
Mingling sighs for the past, with the saddening
    tones of the present.
They, seated near him in love, mark with
    pleasure the smile of the Spirit
Smoothing the wrinkles of age, lightening the
    sternness of nature:
When, as a new-born joy, it wanders, they
    whisper " he slumbers;
Dreams of the dear old times—the dreams of
    his earliest childhood

Come once again—an earnest of peace—a
    balm for his sorrow,
Lifting the weight of his years, off from the
    spirit of Malthus!"
Dreams of the dear old times—now he follows
    the bend of the river
Winding its devious course thro' the meadow
    once owned of his father,
Skirted with copse—a thick undergrowth of
    hazel and dogwood;
Listlessly wandering on, musing of Life and
    the Spirit,
Losing his Soul in a thought so deep it swallows his Being!
Mindless of Earth and the sky, with the
    rippling flow of the waters—
Mindless of mother and home, of sister,
    brother, and father—
Winged of its joy, his Spirit has flown to the
    regions of dreamland!

There, of the gorgeous clouds, it rears a
    temple of glory
Piercing the dark blue vault: glisten the
    myriad spires
Pale as the light of the moon, changing from
    amber to silver,
Shifting their dazzling hues like the glittering
    mass of the iceberg
Jewelled with stars, imprisoned within that
    casket of crystal,
Flashing the pale white light of its radiance
    over the Ocean!

Sad would it be for the Earth were the visions
    of longing eternal;
Closed were her eyes to the measure of time,
    the glories of action.
Soothed by the languishing tones ever whis-
    pering rest to the weary,—

Lulled by the soft laughing flow of raptures,
   deliciously welling
Free from the springs of the heart, weaving
   harmonious numbers,
Winging their way to the regions above, a
   choir of languor,
Up thro' the chasms of night, burdening air
   with their sweetness,—
Closed were the ears of the Soul, to the loftier
   aims of her Being!

Just as a bird of the morn, when aroused by
   the blush of Aurora
Springs from the grass on aerial wings, beat-
   ing music to nature,
Stemming the currents of air, and rising
   higher and higher
Borne far aloft by the wandering gusts which
   buffet his pinions;

Drinking the colorless light of the morning, and steadfastly gazing
Being away, with love for his mate, and her delicate plumage ;—
Yet, in his 'wildering course, a sense of his love, and her nurslings,
Steals like a vision of future into a bosom of longing—
Suddenly wheeling about, he beholds the stream, and the green sward,
This, a mirror of sky reflecting the brightening azure,
That, an emerald mould, and glistening fresh with the dew drops,
Laved with the same fair light he sought in the regions of cloudland:
Swift as a glance of the Sun, he drops from the sky to the meadow—
Thus, from the castles of air, falls to Earth the musings of Malthus!

Turning his pale wan cheek to the stream of
   the light, which, denied him,
Floated a gauze-like veil o'er the shadowy
   Earth and the Heavens,
Sweeping the land and the Sea with its deep-
   ening fringe as of amber,
Trailed by the ministering cloud thro' the
   dust of the ground, and the white mists,
Malthus awakes to the sense of his love, and
   the hope of his blindness!

Wakening thrills of delight in the breast of
   the youth and the maiden,
Softy he calls to the boy and the girl with
   the voice of affection:
"Come to the knees of my age, and ponder
   the words of your father;
Malthus, the blind old man, has something of
   interest to tell you:

Fly to the arms of my age, for I feel you are
    near to my heart's love,—
Ye! ye! alone remain to these arms from the
    forms they have cherished—
Mother and father, with sister and wife—all!
    all! They have left me—
Snatched from the loving embrace, and chilled
    by the breath of the death-fiend!
Daughter—with speed,—in the blush of your
    youth—I long to encircle
Charms which shall draw forth the sigh from
    the languishing breasts of the young
    men,
Youths all alive to the beauties of form in the
    future of Being,
Warmed by the glance of an eye, and thrilled
    by the echoing soft laugh,
Magical, musical—breathing of treasures re-
    served for the loved ones,

Guarded with care by the critical eye of the
    cynical mother!

Such were the years in the past, and I doubt
    not such is the future!
Each age is but to show that the world, with
    its forms, shall continue;
Earth has her robe—the ocean his tides—the
    heart its emotions,
Shifting and surging, and falling perchance,
    but in melody turning
Back to the same old phase that delighted
    the hearts of the Fathers!

Soft is the glance of the Sky to a heart in the
    morning of Being,
Fresh from the hands of the Lord, wakening
    hopes for the future—
Mellow the hum of insect-wing in the tremble
    of motion—

Golden the haze of the dust, deep-tinged with the pencil of sunlight;
Yet, in the end, 'tis the will of the Lord—an end never failing,
Time drags heavily on, till the hope of the future, accomplished,
Dies on the heart of the man, as the leaf on the heart of the forest!

* * * * * *

As they return from the burial ground, the home of the friendless,
See the clouds break up like the mass of ice that covers a river,
Floating in huge-hewn blocks, whilst the still water darkens between them.
Far thro' their cavernous depths behold you the long lost Ether!
Is it the eye of the Lord which brightens and gladdens the landscape?

Circles of blue look down with the passionless
    love-gaze of childhood !

Far over meadow and lea the swift-flitting
    shadows are playing,
Dancing a shadowy-dance—chasing the sun-
    light before them.
Now the Sun marshals his rays behind the
    dark thunder-cloud, looming
Black with impetuous fate, portending tem-
    pestuous ruin :
Ever and anon from behind, peep the glitter-
    ing points of the spear-heads—
Level their shafts—like the glance of an eye
    they haste to the battle !
Heaven's artillery thunders its rage in the
    crash o'er the mountains !
God hurleth his spear in the lightning-dart
    that rendeth the pine trees,

Whilst that from chasm and peak, wild with
    fright, leap the heart-quelling echoes!

Sigheth the Wind of the West, in languish-
    ing numbers and accents:
"I must away, to shepherd the clouds thro'
    the infinite void!"
Like a heart-sigh, it wasteth its life in the
    useless endeavor
By one fell swoop, to sweep from the sky its
    burden of sorrow!
Tho' they move, the dark clouds, tho' they
    lessen and lessen, and fade in the dis-
    tance—
Tho' they curl and divide, and in airy shapes
    lighten the landscape—
The boundless horizon still fleeth and fleeth
    before them;

Thus the heart, tho' relievéd, still nurseth its
    burden of anguish!

*   *   *   *   *   *

"Surely her face is divine, for a spirit-sweet-
    ness descending
Swift from the musical spheres, in its joy has
    fallen upon her,
Gladdening Earth with an angel-smile—a
    power of beauty
Winning the soul unto wisdom, and moving
    the hearts of beholders!

See where she gracefully glides, the perfect
    mould of a woman,
Maidenly veiling her face—fearing the sun-
    light should kiss her!
Panting for bliss, the Wind of the West, with
    the hand of a lover
Gently uptossed the deep-craped veil, disclos-
    ing the features

Homer had sung, as they shone revealed in
    the light of his blindness!
For, when Nature is haze, and eyes formed
    of clay gather blackness,
So that the Sun is an orb of gloom, and the
    tides of the sunbeams
Play o'er the motionless balls upraised to their
    shower of darkness,
Light wells free from the Soul, like a golden
    mist, which, dispersing,
Gladdens the view with emerald meads, and
    vistas of azure
Blending their various tints, to form a glorious union,
Milder by far than the natural eye in its
    vision hath bounded!
Such are the landscapes of mind, and such
    the raptures eternal,—
These are the forms Maeonides saw in peopling Elysium!"

Thus sang the youth in his heart, and these
    are the words which he uttered,
Praising the grace of Amelia, and blessing
    the turf which she trod on,
Whispering low to his friend, "vera incessu
    patuit dea,"—
Venus herself, the praise of the gods, the
    spouse of Hephaistos,
Wandering free in the groves, and suddenly
    chancing upon her,
Paused in the walk, in wonder to gaze on the
    grace of the maiden,—
Staying the step which awakens a thrill in the
    souls of Immortals!

*   *   *   *   *   *

Is it the Air that is whispering thus, on the
    heart of the waters
Sighing, and laughing, and sighing again, as
    they wander forever

Homeless, companionless, rolling in melody
    over the smooth stones—
Such as that shepherd of old had chosen to
    fight with Goliath—
Never to rest, ever losing their stream in the
    gorge of the mountains:
Now reappearing again, and shaping its flight,
    for the Ocean,
Eager, insatiate, longing to swallow Earth,
    Air, and the Heavens;—
Winging its way like a great white bird thro'
    the mists of the forest!

Is it the voice of the Wind, or the pulse of the
    sparkling streamlet
Throbbing in sympathy wild to the call of the
    Sea in the distance,
Murmuring—"Lo, I come!" Singing, "Soon
    and I shall be with you,"

Lost in your froth-capped waves, or spread
    as the foam on the long strand,
Or as the wind-tossed spray, showering light
    on the head of the sailor,
Crowning the slave of his own wild thought
    with the jewels of freedom!

SPRING.

In the Spring! In the Spring!
Earth blushing, renewed,
In her glories renewed,
Caresses her flowers!
They drooped 'neath the rage
Of the pitiless blast;
But the voice of the Wind,
Of the low summer Wind
In melody sighing:
"Awake!"—Whilst the Hours,
Bedecking the bowers,
Responded in soft winning accents:
"Awake! Loved of Heaven, awake!
Remember the past,"—
Has raised Winter's siege!

In the Spring! In the Spring!
Light thoughts sparkle up,
Leap up,—bubble up
From the wells of the heart!
They hang in their lightness
O'er the glass of the stream:
In their rising and falling,
Wakened Memories are calling
To Memories dead—
"Awake joys of heart!
To rhapsody start!
Earth and Heaven are whispering ever:
Awake! Sleep no more!"
Then melt as a dream
That is veiled of its brightness!

ONE'S OWN DAYDREAM.

In the wanderings of Spirit
Isles of beauty, undiscovered
Heretofore by kindred natures,
   Greet the eye:

Clad in robe of waving velvet,
'Chased with violets and roses,
How such tendernesses make us
   Heave the sigh!

Other dream may be for other,
Fair and beautiful as ours—
Sunny lake, and laughing shower;
   Waves of light
Oft in silence lave the long strand
Ruby-red with rolling jewels,

Flashing as the giddy moon-beam
    Reels thro' night!

Other dream may be for other,—
Dream as beautiful as ours—
Losing rhapsody in langour
    Of the soul;

Yet each Spirit loves its own dream,
Calmly moulding its ideal
Pulseless, where the tides of glory
    Ceaseless roll!

Is it that discerning Fancy
Marshals up from heart remembrance
Forms of Being, which to move us
    Crowd each scene,
Thick with wild youth's deathless longings!—
Lost to Spirit, save that visions
Waked of memory 'mid Earth's trials,
    Intervene!—

As the dewy cloud of Evening
Hangs, a rapture, lightly curling
Into tint and smiling notice—
    So with thought!

Would that Soul could dwell forever
'Mid the gay creation floating,
Wafted on mild Music's pinions
    Through the heart!

THE END.

www.ingramcontent.com/pod-product-compliance
Lightning Source LLC
Chambersburg PA
CBHW020903230426
43666CB00008B/1295